Received On

JAN -- 2016

D0753268

NO LONGER PROPERTY OF
SEATTLE PUBLIC LIBRARY

EATING DISORDERS

MENTAL ILLNESSES AND DISORDERS

Alzheimer's Disease

Anxiety Disorders

Attention-Deficit Hyperactivity Disorder

Autism Spectrum Disorders

Bipolar Disorder

Depression

Disruptive Behavior Disorders

Drug and Alcohol Dependence

Eating Disorders

Obsessive-Compulsive Disorder

Post-Traumatic Stress Disorder

Schizophrenia

Sleep Disorders

MENTAL ILLNESSES AND DISORDERS
Awareness and Understanding

EATING
DISORDERS

H.W. Poole

SERIES CONSULTANT

ANNE S. WALTERS, PhD

Chief Psychologist, Emma Pendleton Bradley Hospital

Clinical Associate Professor, Alpert Medical School/Brown University

MASON CREST

Mason Crest
450 Parkway Drive, Suite D
Broomall, PA 19008
www.masoncrest.com

© 2016 by Mason Crest, an imprint of National Highlights, Inc. All rights reserved.
No part of this publication may be reproduced or transmitted in any form or by any
means, electronic or mechanical, including photocopying, recording, taping, or any
information storage and retrieval system, without permission from the publisher.

MTM Publishing, Inc.
435 West 23rd Street, #8C
New York, NY 10011
www.mtmpublishing.com

President: Valerie Tomaselli
Vice President, Book Development: Hilary Poole
Designer: Annemarie Redmond
Copyeditor: Peter Jaskowiak
Editorial Assistant: Andrea St. Aubin

Series ISBN: 978-1-4222-3364-1
ISBN: 978-1-4222-3372-6
Ebook ISBN: 978-1-4222-8573-2

Library of Congress Cataloging-in-Publication Data

Poole, Hilary W., author.
  Eating disorders / by H.W. Poole.
     pages cm. — (Mental illnesses and disorders: awareness and understanding)
  Includes bibliographical references and index.
  ISBN 978-1-4222-3372-6 (hardback) — ISBN 978-1-4222-3364-1 (series) — ISBN 978-1-4222-
8573-2 (ebook)
1. Eating disorders—Juvenile literature. I. Title.
  RC552.E18P66 2016
  616.85'26—dc23
                                  2015006802

Printed and bound in the United States of America.

First printing
9 8 7 6 5 4 3 2 1

TABLE OF CONTENTS

Key Icons to Look for:

Words to Understand: These words with their easy-to-understand definitions will increase the reader's understanding of the text, while building vocabulary skills.

Sidebars: This boxed material within the main text allows readers to build knowledge, gain insights, explore possibilities, and broaden their perspectives by weaving together additional information to provide realistic and holistic perspectives.

Research Projects: Readers are pointed toward areas of further inquiry connected to each chapter. Suggestions are provided for projects that encourage deeper research and analysis.

Text-Dependent Questions: These questions send the reader back to the text for more careful attention to the evidence presented there.

Series Glossary of Key Terms: This back-of-the-book glossary contains terminology used throughout the series. Words found here increase the reader's ability to read and comprehend higher-level books and articles in this field.

People who cope with mental illnesses and disorders deserve our empathy and respect.

(istockphoto/digitalskillet)

Introduction to the Series

According to the National Institute of Mental Health, in 2012 there were an estimated 45 million people in the United States suffering from mental illness, or 19 percent of all US adults. A separate 2011 study found that among children, almost one in five suffer from some form of mental illness or disorder. The nature and level of impairment varies widely. For example, children and adults with anxiety disorders may struggle with a range of symptoms, from a constant state of worry about both real and imagined events to a complete inability to leave the house. Children or adults with schizophrenia might experience periods when the illness is well controlled by medication and therapies, but there may also be times when they must spend time in a hospital for their own safety and the safety of others. For every person with mental illness who makes the news, there are many more who do not, and these are the people that we must learn more about and help to feel accepted, and even welcomed, in this world of diversity.

It is not easy to have a mental illness in this country. Access to mental health services remains a significant issue. Many states and some private insurers have "opted out" of providing sufficient coverage for mental health treatment. This translates to limits on the amount of sessions or frequency of treatment, inadequate rates for providers, and other problems that make it difficult for people to get the care they need.

Meanwhile, stigma about mental illness remains widespread. There are still whispers about "bad parenting," or "the other side of the tracks." The whisperers imply that mental illness is something you bring upon yourself, or something that someone does to you. Obviously, mental illness can be exacerbated by an adverse event such as trauma or parental instability. But there is just as much truth to the biological bases of mental illness. No one is made schizophrenic by ineffective parenting, for example, or by engaging in "wild" behavior as an adolescent. Mental illness is a complex interplay of genes, biology, and the environment, much like many physical illnesses.

People with mental illness are brave soldiers, really. They fight their illness every day, in all of the settings of their lives. When people with an anxiety disorder graduate from college, you know that they worked very hard to get there—harder, perhaps, than those who did not struggle with a psychiatric issue. They got up every day with a pit in their stomach about facing the world, and they worried about their finals more than their classmates. When they had to give a presentation in class, they thought their world was going to end and that they would faint, or worse, in front of everyone. But they fought back, and they kept going. Every day. That's bravery, and that is to be respected and congratulated.

These books were written to help young people get the facts about mental illness. Facts go a long way to dispel stigma. Knowing the facts gives students the opportunity to help others to know and understand. If your student lives with someone with mental illness, these books can help students know a bit more about what to expect. If they are concerned about someone, or even about themselves, these books are meant to provide some answers and a place to start.

The topics covered in this series are those that seem most relevant for middle schoolers—disorders that they are most likely to come into contact with or to be curious about. Schizophrenia is a rare illness, but it is an illness with many misconceptions and inaccurate portrayals in media. Anxiety and depressive disorders, on the other hand, are quite common. Most of our youth have likely had personal experience of anxiety or depression, or knowledge of someone who struggles with these symptoms.

As a teacher or a librarian, thank you for taking part in dispelling myths and bringing facts to your children and students. Thank you for caring about the brave soldiers who live and work with mental illness. These reference books are for all of them, and also for those of us who have the good fortune to work with and know them.

—Anne S. Walters, PhD
Chief Psychologist, Emma Pendleton Bradley Hospital
Clinical Professor, Alpert Medical School/Brown University

CHAPTER ONE

EATING TOO MUCH, EATING TOO LITTLE

Words to Understand

body image: a person's ideas and feelings about his or her body; body images can be positive or negative.

contradictory: several things or ideas that are in conflict with each other.

empathy: understanding someone else's situation and feelings.

epidemic: a widespread illness.

ideal: a standard of perfection.

"Ugh, I'm fat. I need to go on a diet."

You have probably heard someone say this. You may have said it yourself. But was it really true?

Our beliefs about eating and weight can be confusing. On the one hand, more food is available to more people than ever before. Magazines and TV shows about cooking are very popular. Chefs are celebrities. Some people are so interested in fancy dishes that they are called "foodies."

American attitudes about food are confusing. On the one hand, chefs and fine dining seem to be a national obsession . . .

On the other hand, Americans are also eating more unhealthy food than ever before. There are so many overweight people that doctors talk about an "obesity **epidemic**." This means that more people have weight-related health problems too, like diabetes or high cholesterol.

. . . but on the other hand, people are eating more unhealthy fast food than ever before.

Meanwhile, advertising, television, and movies show us super-thin models and stars. But the **ideal** images we see do not have much to do with normal bodies (see box). But this does not stop people from trying to achieve the ideal. According to MarketData Enterprises, Americans spent about $60 billion dollars on weight-loss products and plans in 2013.

FACTS ABOUT BODY IMAGE

- About 85 percent of women say they are unhappy with some aspect of their bodies.
- If you believe what TV shows and advertising say, the "ideal" female body is about 5'11" and weighs about 117 pounds.
- The average woman is about 5'4" and weighs about 140 pounds.
- Only about 5 percent of women actually have the body type that advertisers want us to think is the "ideal" body.

(Adapted from The Refrew Center Foundation, "Learning the Basics: An Introduction to Eating Disorders and Body Image Issues." Available at http://renfrewcenter.com/sites/default/files/LearningTheBasics_AnIntrotoED.pdf.)

And yet some neighborhoods are referred to as "food deserts." In these areas, it is very difficult to buy healthy food. One in five American kids—about 16 million total—go hungry on a regular basis.

It's clear that we have many **contradictory** attitudes about food and weight. For example, most of us like the idea of being rich, so we might want to eat the way wealthy people do. But we are often too busy to cook (and most of us are not rich!). So we end up eating fast food instead. Then we feel guilty and promise to eat healthier tomorrow.

Have you heard the expression, "You are what you eat?" Deep down, we sometimes think that if we eat good food, we are good. If we eat bad food, maybe we are bad. We think that *how we eat* tells us something about *who we are.*

But is that actually true? Does what is on your plate say anything about what is in your heart? Or is a pizza just a pizza?

DID YOU KNOW?

About 95 percent of people who lose weight by dieting will gain the weight back in three years.

Have It Your Way

Americans believe very strongly in the idea of choice. We want the power to make our own decisions. We like to have a lot of choices on TV. We like a lot of choices when we shop. And we like a lot of choices when we eat.

One reason people like choice is because it makes us feel in control. We say, "I want the blue shirt; I don't want the red shirt." Sure, choosing a shirt is a tiny thing. Still, it sends a little signal that we have control over our lives—and that feels good.

Most of the time, wanting to be in control is not a problem. But when our feelings about food get mixed up with our need for control, bad things can start to happen.

There is nothing wrong with wanting to look a certain way. But sometimes people get so focused on ideal bodies that they start to hate their own bodies. They start to believe that their weight relates to their value as humans. Being a thin person can get confused with being a good person.

These feelings can be very upsetting. They can also be dangerous, because they can develop into an eating disorder that can harm or even kill. By some estimates, 24 million Americans suffer from some type of eating disorder.

Although they may not realize it, many people like shopping because it gives them a sense of control.

FREEDOM OF CHOICE?

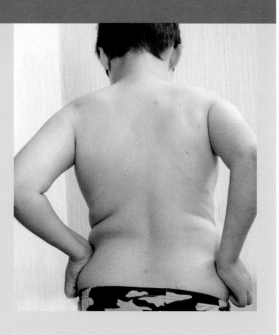

Choice is great. But it is possible to believe in choice too much.

If someone is overweight, we tend to assume it's his or her fault. That person *chose* to eat badly or to not exercise. If that person had more self-control, he or she wouldn't be in that situation. Thinking this way makes us feel better about ourselves. Because, of course, *we* would never make the mistakes *that person* did.

But that overweight person might not have as much choice as you think. For example:

- He might have a type of body that gains weight very easily.
- He might have an illness that causes him to gain weight.
- He might not be able to control what is served for dinner at his house.
- He might need to take medication that causes him to gain weight.
- His family might not have the time or ability to cook healthy food.
- His family might not be able to afford healthy food in the first place.

We all can and should make better choices to improve our health. That's a great goal. In real life, however, choices can be more limited than we want to admit. It's good to have **empathy** for other people rather than judge them.

Experts have several theories about why some people develop eating disorders but others don't. These theories will be discussed later in the book. First, chapter two will look at the types of disorders and talk about what makes one type different from another.

Text-Dependent Questions

1. What are some of our contradictory ideas about food?
2. How much did Americans spend on weight loss in 2013?
3. Why do we like the concept of choice so much?

Research Project

Write down the following in a list:

- your eye color
- your hair color
- your hair style (short, medium, long)
- your height (average, smaller than average, or taller than average)
- your style of dress
- your abilities (what are you best at?)
- your favorite activities or hobbies

Now make the same list for five people you care about.

What do you notice about these lists? Which answers could be changed if someone wanted to? When you look at the list of people you care about, which of the answers are most important to you? What does this tell you about what you value in a person?

CHAPTER TWO

TYPES OF EATING DISORDERS

Words to Understand

atypical: different from what is usually expected.

binge: to do or eat a lot of something in a very short time.

body dysmorphia: constant, negative thoughts about a particular physical flaw; the "flaw" is often something one no one else notices.

fasting: eating nothing at all for a set period of time.

purge: to getting rid of something violently or abruptly.

restrict: to limit sharply.

stereotype: an oversimplified idea about a particular type of person.

Mental illnesses are defined and explained in a book called the *Diagnostic and Statistical Manual of Mental Disorders*, or *DSM-5*; the number five is used because the manual has been updated five times.

According to the *DSM-5*, there are two main types of eating disorders: *anorexia nervosa* and *bulimia nervosa*. (There are several other types, which we will cover at the end of the chapter.)

Anorexia

Anorexia nervosa involves eating far too little, and it can also involve exercising far too much. People with anorexia

Most people with anorexia see themselves as "fat" even when they are dangerously thin.

are starving themselves slowly. They want to get thinner and thinner, but they go way past what the rest of us would consider a healthy, slender body.

Weight is not the only factor, however. While anorexia is partly a physical condition, it is also a mental one. To diagnose the disorder, a doctor will speak to the patient to find out how he *thinks* and *feels* about his body. People with anorexia are extremely fearful of gaining any weight. They are also determined to lose more weight, despite how thin they already are.

Another symptom common among people with anorexia is a "disturbance" in the way they see their bodies. This disturbance is sometimes called **body dysmorphia**, and it involves constant negative thoughts about one's body. For

BODY DYSMORPHIC DISORDER

The symptom of body dysmorphia gives its name to another condition, separate from anorexia, called body dysmorphic disorder (BDD). Someone with BDD has constant negative thoughts about his entire body or one particular body part. The "flaw" may be tiny, or it may not exist at all. But the person with BDD is convinced that the flaw is *huge* and that everyone sees it.

One particular type of BDD happens more in males than females. It's called muscle dysmorphia. People with this disorder get too focused on the size and shape of particular muscle groups. They feel like they can never be "ripped" enough. Muscle dysmorphia can result in eating disorders as well as other unhealthy activities, like steroid use.

Eating disorders and BDD can go hand in hand. But it is important to remember they are not the same. It's possible to have one without the other.

example, someone might measure her hips repeatedly because she fears that they are too wide. For someone with anorexia, body dysmorphia means that she sees herself as overweight, even if she is dangerously underweight.

People with anorexia can be depressed and socially withdrawn. They may lose interest in activities they used to enjoy. They can often be irritable and have trouble sleeping. However, it's not always clear whether these moods are

Ninety-five percent of people with anorexia are under the age of 26.

related to the anorexia. They might be caused by being hungry all the time.

Simply being skinny or not liking food does not necessarily mean that someone has anorexia. Doctors consider both the patient's behavior (such as refusing to eat) and attitude (such as being convinced he is fat when he is not).

Types of Anorexia

There are two types of anorexia nervosa: **binge eating** and **restrictive**.

Anorexia causes problems in many parts of the body. Without nutrients, hair can become brittle and fall out.

SYMPTOMS OF ANOREXIA

How do you know if you or someone you know might have anorexia? These are some common behaviors among people with the disorder. The person:

- believes him or herself to be fat even though he or she is very thin
- talks about food a lot but does not want to eat, especially in front of others
- exercises an extreme amount
- is very focused on body image as proof of worth

As time goes on, physical symptoms start to appear:

- extreme weight loss
- muscle loss
- cold hands and feet
- poor memory
- yellowish skin
- lanugo (a fine layer of hair over the skin)
- brittle bones (osteoporosis)
- disrupted menstrual cycle in girls

Binge Eating. Someone with binge-eating anorexia will eat much more than normal and then **purge** the food. Purging is done by numerous methods: extreme exercise, **fasting**, forcing oneself to vomit, or taking laxatives to get the food out of the body.

Restrictive. Someone with restrictive anorexia severely limits (or **restricts**) the amount of food he or she eats. The person might seem to be fasting almost all the time.

Bulimia Nervosa

The other major type of eating disorder is bulimia nervosa. It involves eating way too much in a short time (bingeing) and then getting rid of the food (purging) through vomiting, fasting, laxatives, or extreme exercise. The *DSM-5* defines bulimia as bingeing and purging at least once a week for at least three months.

Bulimia is somewhat like binge-eating anorexia, but there is a key difference. People with bulimia are of more-or-less average weight. Some people with bulimia might be a bit thinner than you'd expect, and some might be a bit heavier. However, the disorder does not involve starvation in the way that anorexia does.

People with bulimia may not be hungry when they binge. They know they should stop—they may even feel physically uncomfortable—but they can't. They feel "out of control." They often hide food or eat in secret because of the shame they feel. Then they purge to avoid gaining weight.

The physical dangers of anorexia are fairly obvious: people with the disorder risk starving themselves to death. The dangers of bulimia are more subtle, but they are still serious. The human body was not meant to consume large amounts of food and then bring it all back up. Over time, purging can cause many severe health issues, including blood problems, chipped teeth and frequent cavities, tearing the stomach or esophagus, problems with the menstrual cycle in girls, and even heart trouble.

Opposite: Some people with bulimia eat in secret—when everyone else in their house is asleep, for example.

SYMPTOMS OF BULIMIA

Not everyone with bulimia behaves in exactly the same way. However, there are certain habits that are common among people with the disorder. Someone with bulimia will usually:

- have regular episodes of binge eating
- use the bathroom often during and after meals
- use techniques like vomiting, laxatives, or excessive exercise
- overeat in times of stress
- feel like his or her eating is out of control
- focus on weight as proof of personal value

People with bulimia also tend to develop some or all of these physical symptoms:

- cavities and other teeth problems
- dehydration
- broken blood vessels in the eyes
- rashes and pimples

Other Eating Disorders

Although anorexia and bulimia are the best-known eating disorders, a number of other problems can occur.

Binge-Eating Disorder. We have all eaten too much at one time or another. That does not mean we have a disorder. When someone has a binge-eating disorder, episodes of overeating happen often—about once a week for at least three months.

This disorder is like bulimia in some ways. A person with binge-eating disorder will consume more food than would be considered normal and in a short period of time. However, he does not usually follow the bingeing with purging. That's what distinguishes this disorder from bulimia and from the binge-eating type of anorexia.

People with binge-eating disorder feel shame about their eating. They feel a loss of control, much like people with bulimia.

Avoidant/Restrictive Food Intake Disorder. Just as binge-eating disorder is similar to bulimia but not the same, avoidant/restrictive food intake disorder (ARFID) is similar to anorexia but not the same. People with ARFID refuse to eat as much as they need to be healthy. This results in weight loss and nutritional problems. However, people with ARFID do not suffer from the obsessive thoughts about weight or the body dysmorphia that people with anorexia often have. Instead,

EVERYDAY PEOPLE

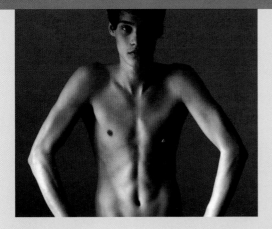

The **stereotype** of a person with anorexia is a white girl in her teens. And many people with eating disorders do fit that description. However, many do not. Eating disorders can happen to people of any race. They can happen to people of any age, and they can happen to any gender. In fact, the number of boys and men with eating disorders is increasing. One Canadian study found that as many as 30 percent of people with anorexia are male.

people with AFRID might refuse to eat because of the food's texture or appearance.

Rumination Disorder. This disorder involves regurgitating food (bringing food back up after it has been swallowed). The food is then either swallowed back down or spit out. The cause of rumination disorder can vary from person to person. Sometimes there's a physical cause, such as a stomach problem, while other times it might be a reaction to stress.

Pica. The disorder called pica involves eating things that are not food, such as sand, dirt, paper, or some other material.

The desire to bring food back up after eating is usually a sign of an eating disorder.

Pica is a disorder in which someone desires to eat non-food items such as sand.

Most babies put strange objects in their mouths, but that is not pica. The babies are just exploring. However, when someone who is old enough to know better keeps eating something that isn't food, she may have pica.

Other Specified Feeding or Eating Disorder (OSFED). The *DSM-5* lists several conditions that qualify as OSFEDs, including:

- **atypical** anorexia nervosa, in which a person has all the symptoms of anorexia but without the weight loss
- night-eating syndrome, in which a person regularly wakes up to eat significant amounts of food
- purging disorder, in which a person purges food, as someone with bulimia would, but does not binge

Unspecified Feeding or Eating Disorder. Doctors use this category when a person has problems related to food but does not fit neatly into any one category.

DID YOU KNOW?

Boys are less likely to get treated for eating disorders because so many people think eating disorders only happen to girls.

Text-Dependent Questions

1. What are the two main types of eating disorders, and what are their symptoms?
2. How is anorexia with bingeing different from bulimia?
3. Name several other eating disorders aside from the main ones.

Research Project

Learn more about one of the eating disorders in this chapter that is interesting to you. Find out about who is at risk for the disorder and why. What are some reasons that people might develop this disorder? How can the disorder be prevented? You might start looking for answers at the research page of the National Eating Disorders Association (http://www.nationaleatingdisorders.org/learn).

CHAPTER THREE

CAUSES OF EATING DISORDERS

 Words to Understand

gene: part of the body that controls how a person develops; our genes are inherited from our parents.

hormone: a substance in the body that helps it function properly.

predisposition: to be more likely to do something, either due to your personality or biology.

EATING DISORDERS IN HISTORY

The term *anorexia nervosa* was coined around 150 years ago. But if we look back in history, we can find examples of the disorder that are even older.

Fasting was once thought to be a path to religious purity. In Europe, it was common to hear stories about young women who could live for months or more without food. Mary I of Scotland, who ruled from 1542 to 1567, is now thought to have had anorexia.

Over time, people came to understand that constantly refusing food was not a miracle but a health concern. A doctor named Sir William Withey Gull, who served as physician to Queen Victoria and England's royal family, gave the disorder its name in 1873.

Mary I of Scotland.

In chapter one, we talked about how society has some confusing attitudes about food, weight, and body image. But those attitudes don't explain why some people have eating disorders. First, even though we are all surrounded by the same attitudes and images, we don't all have eating disorders. Plus, eating disorders have a long history (see box). They have been around a lot longer than our weight-conscious culture.

So the media can't be the only reason. Why do some people develop health problems related to food, while others don't?

There is no simple answer to this question. In fact, there is probably a combination of reasons. The cultural aspect discussed in chapter one may combine with biological and psychological factors.

Biological

Eating disorders are probably caused by problems in the body itself. For example, people with both an eating disorder and depression might have too much of a certain **hormone**. The brains of people with anorexia may have some very basic differences from the brains of those without it.

It is now believed that eating disorders are partly inherited. Someone with an anorexic in her family is about eight times more likely to develop an eating disorder, too.

Most of the time, exercise is great for improving health. However, it is possible for people with eating disorders to overexercise as a way of losing more weight.

No single **gene** determines whether a person gets the disorder or not. However, some people might have a genetic **predisposition** toward it. A few different genes, combined in a particular way, could make it more likely for a person to develop the disorder.

Psychological

Many people with eating disorders begin to have problems when they are teenagers. Because of this, some doctors once believed that the disorders were reactions to the emotional changes of adolescence. A doctor named Hilde Bruch wrote that someone with anorexia "makes her body a stand-in for the life that she can not control."

We now know the causes are not as simple as that. Psychological factors probably do play a role, however. For one thing, many people with eating disorders also have

PERSONALITY AND EATING DISORDERS

There is no single type of person who develops an eating disorder. However, people with eating disorders do sometimes (not always!) have traits in common. These can include:

- low self-esteem
- perfectionism
- a need to please others
- a need for control
- a high level of focus or intensity
- a desire to avoid conflict or negative emotions

BAD ADVICE

If you search online for information on eating disorders, you can easily end up at something called a "thinspiration" website. These sites claim to be nonjudgmental places where people are free to share information about dieting. Instead, they can encourage people to develop a disorder that has a high chance of killing them.

Well-run online support groups are great. It's good to get advice from people who understand your situation. But don't confuse support for your *recovery* with support for your *illness*. A website that encourages you to stop eating is not helping you. It could be hurting you very badly.

body dysmorphia, as discussed earlier. Sometimes people with eating disorders have other problems as well, such as depression or anxiety.

Stress can make the symptoms worse. Sometimes a major life event, such as starting college, can spark the disorder.

Eating disorders are complicated and have more than one cause. A person may be born with a genetic predisposition toward the disorder. Then her personality, family circumstances, or culture may push her in that direction. Lynn Grefe, who leads the National Eating Disorders Association, says

DID YOU KNOW?

In a survey of female college students, about 90 percent of them had gone on a diet at some point. More than 20 percent said they diet often.

that "you're born with a gun and society—your cultural and environmental circumstances—pulls the trigger."

Eating disorders are common among dancers, as well as athletes who play sports with judges (like gymnastics and skating). Sports with referees (like soccer and basketball) tend to inspire fewer eating disorders.

Athletes, Dancers, and Eating Disorders

Kids who play sports or dance have a higher risk of eating disorders than other kids. There are a few reasons for this.

First, these activities put a lot of focus on the body. Athletes may feel they need to be a certain weight to perform well. Or, as happens in ballet or gymnastics, performers may feel pressure to look a certain way.

All the focus on competition creates extra pressure to be perfect. A ballet dancer may try to lose weight right before an

audition. A wrestler might want to drop extra pounds before a meet. This can seem harmless in the short term, but over time, these habits can turn into real health problems.

Athletes and dancers who stay thin are often praised by coaches and parents. Sometimes this creates even more pressure to get even thinner. But studies have shown that thinness does not improve performance as much as you might think. Being healthy and being thin are not necessarily the same.

Text-Dependent Questions

1. Is our culture to blame for eating disorders? Why or why not?
2. What are some possible biological causes of eating disorders?
3. What are some possible psychological causes?
4. Why might someone who looks healthy, like an athlete, still have an eating disorder?

Research Project

Pretend that you are visiting from outer space, and study the media as a true outsider might. Look at commercials, magazines, television shows, and movies. What messages are being sent about food or body image? What do those images tell you about how we think people should look? Or about how we think they should live? Keep a journal with you for a few days, the way a scientist might, and write down what you observe.

CHAPTER FOUR

TREATMENT OF EATING DISORDERS

Words to Understand

comorbidity: two or more illnesses appearing at the same time.

interdisciplinary: involving more than one area of knowledge.

occupational therapist: someone who helps patients learn new skills to address their problems.

outpatient: medical care that happens while a patient continues to live at home.

therapy: treatment of a problem; can be done with medicine or simply by talking with a therapist.

It can be difficult for a person to accept that he or she has an eating disorder. Many people with eating disorders want to be perfect. It's hard for them to hear that they might be hurting themselves.

But as discussed in chapter three, eating disorders can be very dangerous. In fact, anorexia has the highest mortality rate of any mental disorder we know. Without treatment, about 20 percent of people with anorexia will die. But once people seek treatment, that number drops to below 3 percent. That's why it's so important that people with eating disorders get the help they need.

Team Treatment

The American Dietetic Association (ADA) describes eating disorders as "psychiatric disorders with major medical complications." In simpler terms, patients need both medical and psychological care. So, treatment will be

Treating someone with an eating disorder often involves a team of doctors with different specialties.

A dietician can help people with eating disorders learn how to manage their eating in more healthy ways.

interdisciplinary, meaning that it involves doctors from different fields, such as:

- a medical doctor who can perform physical exams and guide the patient's overall health

SUPPORT GROUPS

The National Eating Disorders Association (NEDA) website has lots of information about how to find different kinds of support groups. Some groups even meet online, so that anyone with an Internet connection can join in. The NEDA also has a Navigators program, where volunteers help direct people with eating disorders and their families and friends to resources that can help. (http://www.nationaleatingdisorders.org/neda-navigators)

- a psychiatrist or psychologist who has experience in eating disorders
- an **occupational therapist** who can help the patient learn new skills to cope with daily living
- a dietician who can work with the patient to improve his or her nutrition
- nurses who can monitor the patient's progress, whether in a clinic or at home

Where Does Treatment Happen?

The severity of an eating disorder will determine where a person is treated. If a patient's life is in danger, she will need to be hospitalized. Usually this is just for a short time, while the immediate health problems are addressed.

With treatment, people can recover from eating disorders. However, eating disorders have one of the highest mortality rates of all mental illnesses. It's vital that people with eating disorders get the help they need.

ART AS THERAPY

For some people, eating disorders are a way to cope with painful experiences and feelings. Art therapy can offer a different way to express these feelings. Drawing, painting, or sculpture might help patients communicate what they are going through.

Some eating disorder clinics have art therapy programs. There are also independent art therapy programs in many urban areas. The American Art Therapy Association has an online "therapist locator" that can help connect you with someone in your area.

Art therapy alone is *not* enough to resolve an eating disorder. But it is worth considering as part of larger treatment plan.

Sometimes people are treated in clinics that specialize in eating disorders. Patients may stay in a clinic for a few days, weeks, or months. Some treatments take place in a "partial hospital" setting, which means that people are in the program during the day and then go home at night. That way, they can practice new skills with family and friends.

Much of the treatment for eating disorders happens on an **outpatient** basis. A patient might have regular meetings in a therapist's office, or a social worker might visit the patient at home. Group **therapy**, in which several patients get together to talk about their problems, can also be very useful. It helps patients realize they are not alone.

What about Drugs?

There is no pill that makes eating disorders go away. However, because it is so common for people with eating disorders to also have depression or anxiety, sometimes doctors do prescribe medicine to help with those other issues.

An antidepressant such as fluoxetine (brand name: Prozac) is sometimes given to patients with eating disorders. However, fluoxetine can cause some patients to lose more weight—a terrible side effect for someone with anorexia. It's important to discuss all options and side effects with your doctor.

Nearly half of the people with eating disorders are also suffering from depression.

Eating Disorders and Other Mental Disorders

It is common for people with eating disorders to have other mental disorders as well. This is called **comorbidity**. People with anorexia or bulimia may also suffer from depression, extreme anxiety, body dysmorphia, or obsessive-compulsive disorder.

It can be tricky to separate out these different problems, because they are closely related. A patient might start with an eating disorder but then become anxious and depressed as the disorder gets worse. In this case a doctor might focus on the eating disorder first, and then deal with the depression. Or, sometimes the depression is treated with medicine, while the eating disorder is treated with therapy.

Sometimes the other disorder comes first and the eating disorder comes second. For example, if someone suffers abuse

A team of medical professionals can help people recover from anorexia.

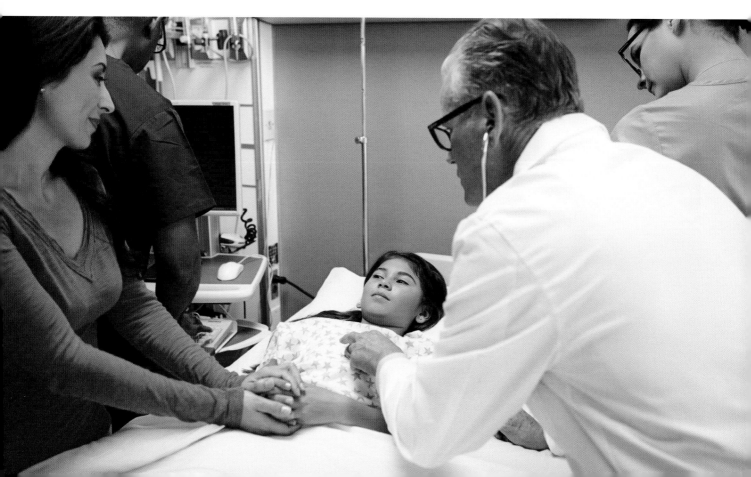

FIND OUT MORE

For more information on some of the problems that can occur along with eating disorders, you might want to read other books in this set:

- *Anxiety Disorders*
- *Bipolar Disorder*
- *Depression*
- *Obsessive-Compulsive Disorder*

as a child, she might develop post-traumatic stress disorder (PTSD). She might act out her anxiety by refusing to eat. An eating disorder can develop from there. In that case, a doctor might treat the PTSD first, and the eating disorder might start to improve as the patient feels better.

Text-Based Questions

1. What kinds of doctors might help treat someone with an eating disorder?
2. Where will treatment take place?
3. What other illnesses can complicate eating disorders?

Research Project

Experiment with the basics of art therapy. Think about different colors and how each makes you feel certain ways. Also consider different types of lines—straight lines, jagged lines, and so on.

Make two drawings: one that looks like how you feel when you are happy, and one that looks like how you feel when you are sad. When you are done, write down what it felt like to make these pictures. How do you think this experience might help someone who is in therapy?

Further Reading

BOOKS

Kolodny, Nancy J. *The Beginner's Guide to Eating Disorders Recovery.* Carlsbad, CA: Gurze Books, 2004.

Nelson, Tammy. *What's Eating You?: A Workbook for Teens with Anorexia, Bulimia, and Other Eating Disorders.* Oakland, CA: New Harbinger Publications, 2008.

Orr, Tamra. *When the Mirror Lies: Anorexia, Bulimia, and Other Eating Disorders.* Danbury, CT: Franklin Watts, 2007.

Osgood, Kelsey. *How to Disappear Completely: On Modern Anorexia.* New York: Overlook Press, 2014.

ONLINE

Kids Health. "Eating Disorders."
http://kidshealth.org/teen/food_fitness/problems/eat_disorder.html.

National Eating Disorders Association.
http://www.nationaleatingdisorders.org/.

National Institute of Mental Health: Eating Disorders.
http://www.nimh.nih.gov/health/topics/eating-disorders/index.shtml.

LOSING HOPE?

This free, confidential phone number will connect you to counselors who can help.

The National Eating Disorders Association
1-800-931-2237

Series Glossary

acute: happening powerfully for a short period of time.

affect: as a noun, the way someone seems on the outside—including attitude, emotion, and voice (pronounced with the emphasis on the first syllable, "AFF-eckt").

atypical: different from what is usually expected.

bipolar: involving two, opposite ends.

chronic: happening again and again over a long period of time.

comorbidity: two or more illnesses appearing at the same time.

correlation: a relationship or connection.

delusion: a false belief with no connection to reality.

dementia: a mental disorder, featuring severe memory loss.

denial: refusal to admit that there is a problem.

depressant: a substance that slows down bodily functions.

depression: a feeling of hopelessness and lack of energy.

deprivation: a hurtful lack of something important.

diagnose: to identify a problem.

empathy: understanding someone else's situation and feelings.

epidemic: a widespread illness.

euphoria: a feeling of extreme, even overwhelming, happiness.

hallucination: something a person sees or hears that is not really there.

heredity: the passing of a trait from parents to children.

hormone: a substance in the body that helps it function properly.

hypnotic: a type of drug that causes sleep.

impulsivity: the tendency to act without thinking.

inattention: distraction; not paying attention.

insomnia: inability to fall asleep and/or stay asleep.

licensed: having an official document proving one is capable with a certain set of skills.

manic: a high level of excitement or energy.

misdiagnose: to incorrectly identify a problem.

moderation: limited in amount, not extreme.

noncompliance: refusing to follow rules or do as instructed.

onset: the beginning of something; pronounced like "on" and "set."

outpatient: medical care that happens while a patient continues to live at home.

overdiagnose: to determine more people have a certain illness than actually do.

pediatricians: doctors who treat children and young adults.

perception: awareness or understanding of reality.

practitioner: a person who actively participates in a particular field.

predisposition: to be more likely to do something, either due to your personality or biology.

psychiatric: having to do with mental illness.

psychiatrist: a medical doctor who specializes in mental disorders.

psychoactive: something that has an effect on the mind and behavior.

psychosis: a severe mental disorder where the person loses touch with reality.

psychosocial: the interaction between someone's thoughts and the outside world of relationships.

psychotherapy: treatment for mental disorders.

relapse: getting worse after a period of getting better.

spectrum: a range; in medicine, from less extreme to more extreme.

stereotype: a simplified idea about a type of person, not connected to actual individuals.

stimulant: a substance that speeds up bodily functions.

therapy: treatment of a problem; can be done with medicine or simply by talking with a therapist.

trigger: something that causes something else.

Index

Page numbers in *italics* refer to photographs.

About the Author

H. W. POOLE is a writer and editor of books for young people, such as the *Horrors of History* series (Charlesbridge). She is also responsible for many critically acclaimed reference books, including *Political Handbook of the World* (CQ Press) and the *Encyclopedia of Terrorism* (SAGE). She was coauthor and editor of the *History of the Internet* (ABC-CLIO), which won the 2000 American Library Association RUSA award.

About the Advisor

ANNE S. WALTERS is Clinical Associate Professor of Psychiatry and Human Behavior. She is the Clinical Director of the Children's Partial Hospital Program at Bradley Hospital, a program that provides partial hospital level of care for children ages 7–12 and their families. She also serves as Chief Psychologist for Bradley Hospital. She is actively involved in teaching activities within the Clinical Psychology Training Programs of the Alpert Medical School of Brown University and serves as Child Track Seminar Co-Coordinator. Dr. Walters completed her undergraduate work at Duke University, graduate school at Georgia State University, internship at UTexas Health Science Center, and postdoctoral fellowship at Brown University. Her interests lie in the area of program development, treatment of severe psychiatric disorders in children, and psychotic spectrum disorders.

Photo Credits

Photos are for illustrative purposes only; individuals depicted in the photos, both on the cover and throughout this book, are only models.

Cover Photo: iStock.com/Scrofula

Dollar Photo Club: 13 Monkey Business; 14 olegmalyshev; 17 Tatty; 20 Barabas Attila; 23 Кирилл Рыжов; 24 Africa Studio; 25 iulianvalentin; 27 juliaphoto; 30 Georgios Kollidas; 31 studio1901; 33 Focus Pocus LTD; 34 danr13; 37 Minerva Studio; 39 Monkey Business; 40 rgvc; 42 Monkey Business. **iStock.com:** 10 4774344sean; 11 JulNichols; 19 Scrofula; 26 b-d-s; 38 Fertnig; 41 DragonImages.